HARD-TO-BEAT
SPORTS RECORDS

BY BARRY WILNER

THE WILD WORLD OF
SPORTS

SportsZone

...print of Abdo Publishing
...bdopublishing.com

abdopublishing.com

Published by Abdo Publishing, a division of ABDO, PO Box 398166, Minneapolis, Minnesota 55439.
Copyright © 2018 by Abdo Consulting Group, Inc. International copyrights reserved in all countries.
No part of this book may be reproduced in any form without written permission from the publisher.
SportsZone™ is a trademark and logo of Abdo Publishing.

Printed in the United States of America, North Mankato, Minnesota
102017
012018

Cover Photo: Paul Battaglia/AP Images, foreground; Jeff Roberson/AP Images, background
Interior Photos: Hulton Archive/Getty Images, 4; AP Images, 7, 8, 8–9, 25, 29, 30, 34, 42–43; Richard
Sheinwald/AP Images, 10; Ed Kolenovsky/AP Images, 12; Jerry W. Hoefer/Fort Worth Star-Telegraph/AP
Images, 13; Denis Paquin/AP Images, 15; Paul Spinelli/AP Images, 17; Four Seam Images/AP Images, 18;
Denis Poroy/AP Images, 20; Keith Srakocic/AP Images, 21; Paul Vathis/AP Images, 23; Michael Conroy/AP
Images, 26; Bruce Bennett/Getty Images, 33; Wa Funches/AP Images, 35; Martin Meissner/AP Images, 37;
Elise Amendola/AP Images, 38; Lenny Ignelzi/AP Images, 40; Mark J. Terrill/AP Images, 40–41; Lou Krasky/
AP Images, 44; Chris O'Meara/AP Images, 45

Editor: Patrick Donnelly
Series Designer: Craig Hinton

Publisher's Cataloging-in-Publication Data

Names: Wilner, Barry, author.
Title: Hard-to-beat sports records / by Barry Wilner.
Description: Minneapolis, Minnesota : Abdo Publishing, 2018. | Series: The wild world of sports | Includes
      online resources and index.
Identifiers: LCCN 2017946930 | ISBN 9781532113659 (lib.bdg.) | ISBN 9781532152535 (ebook)
Subjects: LCSH: Sports Records--Juvenile literature. | Sports and history--Juvenile literature. | Records--
      Juvenile literature.
Classification: DDC 796.021--dc23
LC record available at https://lccn.loc.gov/2017946930

TABLE OF
CONTENTS

MOUND MASTERY

Cy Young wouldn't have been a great fit in modern baseball. These days, pitchers rarely throw complete games. But when Young played, pitchers were expected to throw all nine innings—or more, if necessary. And they often pitched on one or two days' rest. That led to some amazing statistics that likely will never be topped.

For example, from 1890 to 1911 Young started a record 815 games. He finished 749 of them. No one has come within 100 of that remarkable complete-game total. And Young's 7,356 career innings pitched put him more than 1,300 ahead of Pud Galvin, who was second.

Young's 511 victories put him 94 ahead of the next-closest pitcher, Walter Johnson. Young won at least 30 games in five different seasons. He also lost 316 games, another record, though that is only six more losses than Galvin's total, even though Young pitched for seven more seasons.

Cy Young set the bar high for future pitchers.

THE STREAK

Joe DiMaggio was known as one of the most consistent players in Major League Baseball (MLB) history. Hitting, fielding, base running—anything a ballplayer could do, DiMaggio was among the best. But even fans of the New York Yankees center fielder had to be amazed when he got a hit in 56 consecutive games. It's widely considered one of the greatest streaks in sports history.

The streak began with a humble 1-for-4 effort against the Chicago White Sox on May 15, 1941. Then, every game for the next two months, he put at least one hit into the scorebook.

Four times during the streak, DiMaggio had four hits in a game. But there also were some close calls; he had one hit in 34 of the games.

In Game 36, DiMaggio was hitless through six innings. St. Louis Browns manager Luke Sewell ordered Bob Muncrief to walk DiMaggio in his next at-bat. A walk doesn't count as a hit, and the

Joe DiMaggio lashes a base hit to extend his hitting streak to 42 games on June 29, 1941.

DiMaggio, *second from right*, is congratulated by Yankees manager Joe McCarthy and his teammates after Game 42 of his streak.

streak likely would have been snapped. Muncrief said no, Sewell backed off, and DiMaggio singled.

The streak ended on July 17 in front of 67,468 fans at Cleveland, where third baseman Ken Keltner robbed DiMaggio of sure hits in the first and seventh innings. DiMaggio grounded into a double play in the eighth inning. When the Yankees closed out a 4–3 victory, the streak was over.

DiMaggio hit .408 during the streak, going 91-for-223 with 15 home runs and 55 runs batted in (RBIs). But the humble hero likely would've been happier to point out that the Yankees went 41–13 (with two ties that counted as games) over that stretch. DiMaggio shattered the previous hitting streak record of 45 games set by Willie Keeler in 1896–97. And the closest anyone has come to matching DiMaggio was in 1978, when Pete Rose hit in 44 straight games.

DiMaggio singles to extend his streak to 44 games on July 1, 1941.

CHAPTER 3

NO-HIT NOLAN

When Nolan Ryan was a wild young pitcher for the New York Mets, he made batters nervous. They didn't know where the ball was headed—over the plate, in the dirt, or maybe even between their ribs.

But Ryan kept working, and soon he had perfected his craft. So every time he took the mound, fans, teammates, opponents—and often Ryan himself—believed a no-hitter was possible.

Seven times, they were right. Ryan also threw 12 complete-game one-hitters. Both are MLB records.

He was nicknamed "The Ryan Express" because his wicked fastball seemed like a train bearing down on home plate. Baseball's all-time strikeouts king whiffed 5,714 batters, nearly 1,000 more than anyone else. And he was unhittable in some games.

Ryan's first no-hitter came in 1973 for the California Angels. He struck out 12 Kansas City Royals in a 3–0 victory. Two months later,

Nolan Ryan throws a pitch in Detroit on July 15, 1973, during his second career no-hitter.

he did it again, this time with 17 strikeouts against the Detroit Tigers. Only six pitchers have had two no-hitters in a season.

Ryan threw two more no-hitters over the next two seasons and added a fifth in 1981 while pitching for the Houston Astros. That set the MLB record for most career no-hitters.

But he kept going, adding to his legend with the Texas Rangers by pitching his sixth no-hitter in 1990. For his final masterpiece he struck out 16 Toronto Blue Jays on May 1, 1991, posting his seventh no-hitter at age 44.

Hall of Fame slugger Reggie Jackson likely summed up the thoughts of many players regarding the flamethrower. "Ryan's the only guy who put fear in me," Jackson said. "Not because he could get me out, but because he could kill me. You just hoped to mix in a walk so you could have a good night and go 0-for-3."

Ryan fires a fastball on September 26, 1981, when he no-hit the Los Angeles Dodgers.

BACK-TO-BACK

Even with all of his no-hitters, Nolan Ryan never did what Johnny Vander Meer did in 1938. The Cincinnati Reds left-hander no-hit the Boston Braves on June 11. Four days later, in the first night game ever at Ebbets Field in Brooklyn, he held the Dodgers hitless. That's the only time a pitcher has thrown back-to-back no-hitters in MLB history.

EVERYDAY PLAYER

Yankees first baseman Lou Gehrig played in 2,130 straight games, a streak that seemed untouchable when it ended in 1939.

Then along came Cal Ripken Jr., who played in every Baltimore Orioles game from May 30, 1982, until September 19, 1998. That's 2,632 games in a row.

The Hall of Fame shortstop surpassed Gehrig's record on September 6, 1995, in front of his hometown fans at Oriole Park at Camden Yards. Ripken's teammates pushed him out of the dugout to run a victory lap. He also had two hits, including a home run, in the Orioles' 4–2 victory over the California Angels.

Ripken kept the streak going for another three years, although he did switch from shortstop to third base. When he finally sat out, he did it without fanfare or drama. He simply told manager Ray Miller not to put him in the lineup.

"It was time," Ripken said.

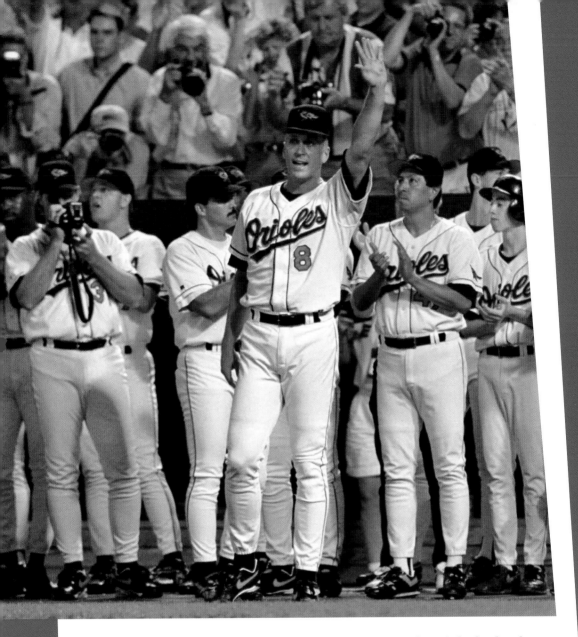

Cal Ripken Jr. waves to the home crowd on the night he broke Lou Gehrig's record for consecutive games played.

The closest any MLB player has come to Ripken's streak since then was when shortstop Miguel Tejada played in 1,152 straight games from 2000 to 2007.

THROW ME THE BALL

Many wide receivers in the National Football League (NFL) have a reputation for showboating. They often appear to be more interested in making the highlight shows or going viral with their touchdown dances.

All Jerry Rice cared about was catching the ball.

Once voted the best player in NFL history by NFL Network, Rice caught 1,549 passes in his 20 pro seasons. That's 224 more receptions than anyone else. He scored 208 career touchdowns, 33 more than any other NFL player.

Most incredible, though, was his total of 22,895 receiving yards. That's almost 7,000 yards more than his former teammate Terrell Owens in second place. The best wide receivers in a given season might gain 1,300 yards. They'd have to do that for 18 years to top the three-time Super Bowl winner.

Jerry Rice made a lot of catches, but he also used his elite speed to increase his yardage total.

Rice played 16 seasons with the San Francisco 49ers. He wasn't the fastest receiver in the league. But he made sharp cuts, had glue-like hands, and ran perfect routes. And with the ball in his hands, Rice was uncatchable.

MR. RELIABLE

Football is a rugged game. Quarterbacks take a pounding. But Brett Favre started 321 straight games. Every week from 1992 to 2010—including playoff games—Favre was under center, taking the first snap of the game for the Green Bay Packers, the New York Jets, or the Minnesota Vikings.

"I've always assumed I'd play every game," Favre once said, explaining the mentality that allowed him to set an NFL record for position players.

Favre's streak is nearly 100 games longer than that of any other quarterback. It began in September 1992. Favre was a second-year player backing up Packers starter Don Majkowski. When Majkowski injured his ankle in Week 3 against the Cincinnati Bengals at Lambeau Field, Favre came in and rallied the Packers to victory.

Favre started the next week, and every week after that, for the next 18 years.

Brett Favre started his streak with the Green Bay Packers in 1992.

19

Favre spent the 2008 season with the New York Jets, starting all 16 games as usual.

He didn't miss a game until a shoulder injury was too painful for him to play for Minnesota in December 2010. He was injured the week before in a game against Buffalo. The Bills' Arthur Moats hit him square in the back and Favre fell to the turf, done for the day. A few weeks later, his Hall of Fame career was over.

What made Favre so special? His toughness, for sure. He would stay in the passing pocket longer than most quarterbacks, waiting for a receiver to get open. He took some big hits from much larger defenders. Favre was sacked an incredible 525 times in his career.

And don't forget his ability to play in pain. Favre injured pretty much every part of his body, but he never asked for a day off. He once played with a broken bone in his foot. Another time, he was out there with 10 stitches in his chin. Sometimes Favre could barely bend his elbow during the week. But on Sunday, he was right back out there.

"I had a blast," Favre said when he was inducted into the Pro Football Hall of Fame in 2016. "And I think anyone who watched me play would say that."

Favre finished his career by playing two seasons with the Minnesota Vikings.

WILT'S 100

Before they became the Golden State Warriors, the team called Philadelphia home. In those days the Warriors played a few games every season in Hershey, Pennsylvania. On March 2, 1962, against the New York Knicks in Hershey, 7-foot-1-inch center Wilt Chamberlain of the Warriors had a game for the ages.

Chamberlain had 41 points at halftime. When he added 28 in the third quarter, the fans began sensing history. So did the Knicks. They began fouling Chamberlain every time he got the ball. "Wilt the Stilt" was normally a bad free-throw shooter. But that night, he made an amazing 28 of 32 shots from the line.

Early in the fourth quarter, Chamberlain surpassed the previous scoring record of 78 points, which he had set just three months earlier. Then, with 46 seconds left, he made a short shot to reach 100 points. Fans streamed onto the court to celebrate a feat they likely knew they'd never see again. The only player ever to come close to that was Kobe Bryant of the Los Angeles Lakers. He scored 81 points in a 2006 game against the Toronto Raptors.

Wilt Chamberlain poses with a sign indicating his 100 points against the New York Knicks on March 2, 1962.

CHAMPION BRUINS

I t's difficult for college basketball teams to win back-to-back National Collegiate Athletic Association (NCAA) championships. So it's incredible that coach John Wooden's University of California, Los Angeles (UCLA) Bruins won seven straight men's basketball titles.

Known as the "Wizard of Westwood," Wooden was a brilliant coach and recruiter. During the string of championships (1967 to 1973), Hall of Famers Lew Alcindor (now Kareem Abdul-Jabbar), Bill Walton, and Keith (now Jamaal) Wilkes were just a few of the All-Americans who played for the Bruins.

During the championship streak, the closest score in a championship game was a five-point win over Florida State University in 1972. One of the biggest wins in UCLA's title run was a revenge game at the Final Four. In January 1968, the University of Houston had upset the Bruins 71–69. It was called "The Game of the Century," with 52,693 fans watching at the Houston Astrodome.

John Wooden holds the NCAA championship trophy after UCLA won the 1971 national title.

UCLA got revenge a couple of months later in the Final Four, when they whipped the Cougars 101–69 in the national semifinals. Then the Bruins beat the University of North Carolina to win the 1967–68 crown.

UNBEATABLE UCONN

How much do the University of Connecticut (UConn) women's basketball players hate losing? After falling 88–86 in overtime at Stanford University in November 2014, UConn went two and a half years before tasting defeat again.

The Huskies won 111 straight games, including NCAA championships in 2015 and 2016. Most amazing was what they did in the 2016–17 season. The Huskies graduated three All-Americans, including three-time NCAA Player of the Year Breanna Stewart. Coach Geno Auriemma expected to lose a few games with a young team. Instead, UConn won all 32 regular-season contests and their first four in the postseason. Only three victories were closer than 10 points, and UConn scored 90 points or more 19 times.

When the Huskies lost in the Final Four to Mississippi State, it was one of the biggest upsets in women's basketball history. But all that meant was the Huskies had to get to work on another streak.

Morgan Tuck (3), Kia Nurse (11), and Breanna Stewart (30) celebrate UConn's victory in the 2016 national title game.

QUICKIE HAT TRICK

Bill Mosienko wasn't one of hockey's greatest scorers. Except, that is, on March 23, 1952.

The Chicago Blackhawks forward had said a few days earlier that he would like to be in the National Hockey League (NHL) record books. Then, against the New York Rangers at Madison Square Garden, Mosienko made his wish come true.

The Blackhawks trailed 6–2 when Mosienko beat Rangers third-string goalie Lorne Anderson at 6:09 of the third period. He skated through the defense to score again at 6:20. Chicago won the next faceoff, teammate George Gee fed Mosienko at the net, and the Blackhawks' captain completed his hat trick, all within 21 seconds.

He almost made it four goals in 28 seconds. Chicago won the next faceoff, too, and Mosienko fired a shot that hit the goalpost.

Bill Mosienko had a lot to smile about after he scored the fastest hat trick in NHL history.

The Blackhawks rallied to win 7–6. Afterward, Mosienko posed for photographers holding three pucks in his right hand and his can't-miss stick in his left. Since that night, the quickest hat trick in the NHL has been 44 seconds by Jean Beliveau of the Montreal Canadiens in 1955.

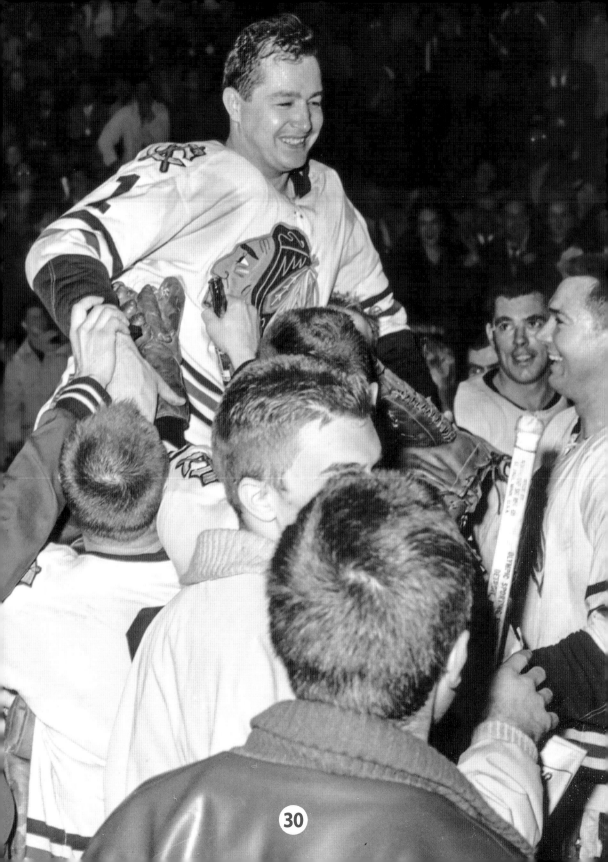

HALL GETS THE CALL

Until late in the 1960s, NHL teams usually used one goaltender for most of the season. Sometimes, the team trainer served as the backup.

There was no question who would guard the net for the Detroit Red Wings and then for the Chicago Blackhawks from 1955 to 1962. Glenn Hall started 502 consecutive games during that stretch.

Hall, who won the NHL Rookie of the Year Award in 1955–56, began the streak when he replaced another Hall of Fame goalie, Terry Sawchuk, in Detroit. He started all 70 games the next season for Detroit, including one playoff game during which he suffered a cut to the face. He received 26 stitches and returned to the ice.

In 1957 Hall was traded to Chicago, where he started every game for five more seasons and won the Stanley Cup in 1961. He later helped the expansion St. Louis Blues reach the Stanley Cup Final in their first two seasons. Hall retired in 1971 at the age of 39 and through 2017 remained in the top 10 in career wins, shutouts, and minutes played.

Glenn Hall gets a ride off the ice after helping the Chicago Blackhawks clinch the Stanley Cup in 1961.

GRETZKY'S
AMAZING SEASON

They called him "The Great One," and not just because the moniker fit so well with his last name. Wayne Gretzky was a superstar while still a teenager. By the end of his 21-season career, he owned every important scoring record in hockey. He also won four Stanley Cups, and his No. 99 was retired throughout the NHL.

Gretzky's greatest feat among so many was scoring 212 points during the 1981–82 season with the Edmonton Oilers. He was only 21 years old when he scored an NHL-record 92 goals and added 120 assists. Gretzky had a hand in half of the Oilers' goals that season.

He scored 50 goals in the first 39 games of the schedule, reaching 50 with five goals in Edmonton's 39th game. The previous record had

Wayne Gretzky heads up the ice for the Edmonton Oilers.

Gretzky splits the Los Angeles Kings' defense.

been 50 goals in 50 games. In the first 50 games that season, Gretzky scored 61 goals.

Gretzky had 10 hat tricks and a league-leading six short-handed goals that season. He had at least one point in all but eight Oilers games. And he finished 65 points ahead of fellow Hall of Famer Mike Bossy. And that's saying something: Bossy's career-high 147 points was the third-highest total ever for an NHL player at that point.

With Gretzky as their leader, the Oilers became one of the NHL's top teams in 1981–82. But they were upset by the Los Angeles Kings in the first round of the playoffs, despite Gretzky recording 12 points in that five-game series.

Oddly, Gretzky was not the fastest skater on his team. Paul Coffey was. Gretzky didn't have the hardest shot, either. That honor belonged to Jari Kurri. Mark Messier, not Gretzky, was the toughest player.

But Gretzky was simply the greatest. He seemed to see the game in slow motion. He knew where to go before anyone else did. He often stood behind the net with the puck, a new strategy at the time. From there, he could set up teammates or make a move himself to get in scoring position.

"A good hockey player plays where the puck is," Gretzky once said. "A great hockey player plays where the puck is going to be."

Gretzky fights off New York Islanders defenseman Denis Potvin.

GOLDEN BOY

Michael Phelps slashed through the water like a barracuda and gobbled up gold medals along the way. Backstroke, butterfly, breaststroke, or freestyle—it didn't matter to the American swimming legend. From the age of 19 to 31, nearly everything Phelps touched in the swimming pool turned to gold.

The most decorated athlete in Olympic history won 28 medals, 23 of them gold. Soviet gymnast Larisa Latynina held the previous record with 18 medals. And Phelps set plenty of world records along the way.

Phelps won six gold and two bronze medals at the 2004 Games in Athens, Greece. Four years later he won a record eight gold medals in Beijing, China.

In 2012 Phelps brought home four gold and two silver medals at the Games in London, England. And finally, after considering

No Olympic athlete has won more medals than US swimmer Michael Phelps.

retirement, he came back for the 2016 Olympics in Rio de Janeiro, Brazil, where he won five gold medals and one silver medal.

Phelps romped in some races. In others, he won by a fingertip. He always gave his all.

"I want to be able to look back and say, 'I've done everything I can, and I was successful,'" Phelps said. "I don't want to look back and say, 'I should have done this or that.'"

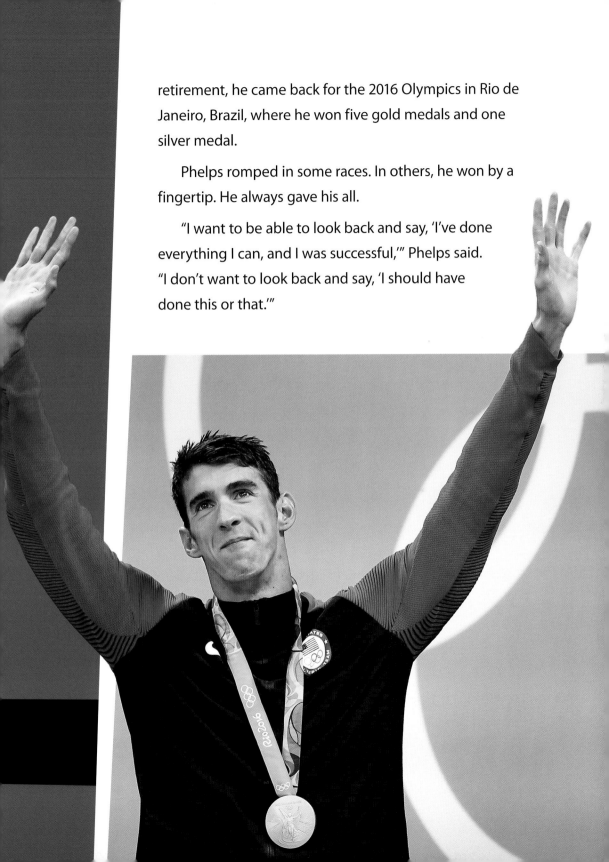

PEBBLE BEACH
ROMP

The US Open is the toughest test in golf. It is played each year on one of the country's most difficult courses. The greens are slick, the rough is long, and the pressure is high.

In 2000, at Pebble Beach, California, along the scenic Pacific coast, Tiger Woods ignored all of those distractions. He won his first US Open by a jaw-dropping 15 strokes.

Woods had already won two other golf majors. He took the Masters by an unbelievable 12 strokes in 1997 and edged Sergio Garcia by one stroke to win the 1999 PGA Championship.

But what he did at Pebble Beach was magical.

His drives from the tee were long and straight down the fairways, from his first shot of the week through the 72nd hole. Nearly all of his

Tiger Woods shows off the winner's trophy after dominating the 2000 US Open at Pebble Beach Golf Links.

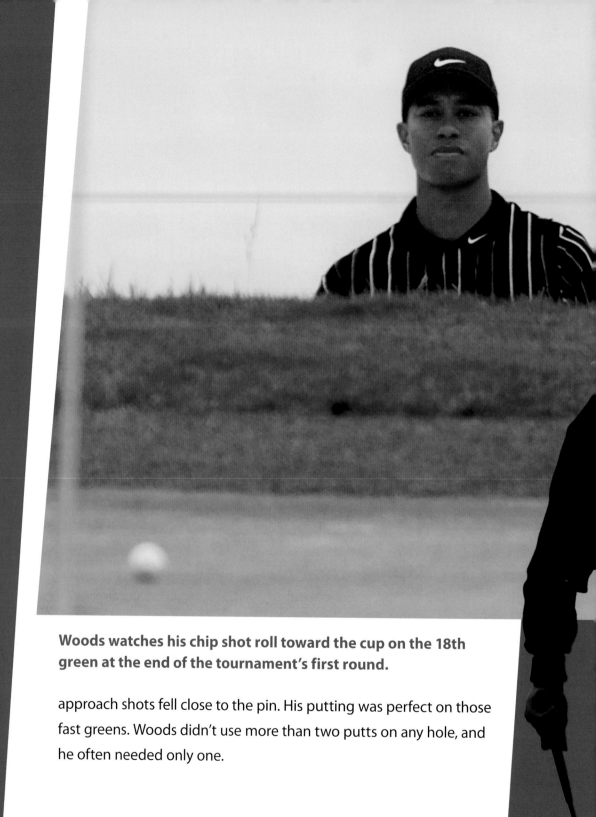

Woods watches his chip shot roll toward the cup on the 18th green at the end of the tournament's first round.

approach shots fell close to the pin. His putting was perfect on those fast greens. Woods didn't use more than two putts on any hole, and he often needed only one.

On a par-71 layout at Pebble Beach, Woods posted scores of 65–69–71–67. His 272 total was 12 shots under par. The next best score was 3 over. The previous best US Open final score was 8 under.

Woods led through every round. His 6-stroke lead after the second round was the largest ever. So was his 10-stroke lead after 54 holes. Whipping winds on Saturday caused him to shoot even-par 71, but only one golfer broke par all day, and Woods gained four strokes on the field.

This victory began the "Tiger Slam." When a player wins all four majors (the British Open is the other) in a calendar year, it's called a Grand Slam. Woods didn't accomplish that, but he followed the victory at Pebble Beach by winning the British Open and PGA in 2000 and the Masters in 2001.

"Tiger has raised the bar," said Tom Watson, winner of the 1982 US Open at Pebble Beach. "And it seems that he's the only guy who can jump over that bar."

Woods ran away from the pack with his record-setting victory.

41

KING
OF THE ROAD

Most auto races end with the winner getting the checkered flag. In the history of American stock car racing, only two drivers have collected at least 100 of them. Topping the list is "The King," Richard Petty, with 200 victories, 95 more than runner-up David Pearson.

Petty followed his father, Lee, onto the racetrack. Lee, also a Hall of Fame driver, won 54 races. It took Richard less than 10 years on NASCAR's top circuit to beat that.

Racing has always been a family affair for the Pettys. Richard's brother Maurice was his crew chief and engineer and had also worked for their father. Richard's son Kyle, who went on to drive the blue

Richard Petty is all smiles after winning a race in 1970.

Until Jimmie Johnson came along in the blue No. 48 Chevrolet, no NASCAR driver had won more than two consecutive season championships. Then Johnson won the title in 2006, and again in 2007, 2008, 2009, and 2010—five in a row. He added championships in 2013 and 2016, tying the record of seven set by Richard Petty and Dale Earnhardt Sr.

No. 43 car after Richard retired, was an eight-time winner for Richard Petty Motorsports.

The King was at his best in 1967, when he won 27 of the 49 races. The mark likely will never be touched now that the season has been shortened to 36 events.

Petty was a driver who would race anywhere at any time. On dirt tracks or pavement. On two-mile raceways or half-mile tracks. In big cities such as Atlanta or small towns like Hickory, North Carolina, near where he grew up. Fans loved him everywhere.

NASCAR's biggest race is the Daytona 500 in Florida. It opens each season. Petty won it seven times, also a record.

Petty's last win came in the Firecracker 400 on July 4, 1984, at Daytona Speedway, with President Ronald Reagan on hand.

Petty acknowledges the fans before the Daytona 500 in 1992, his last year on the NASCAR circuit.

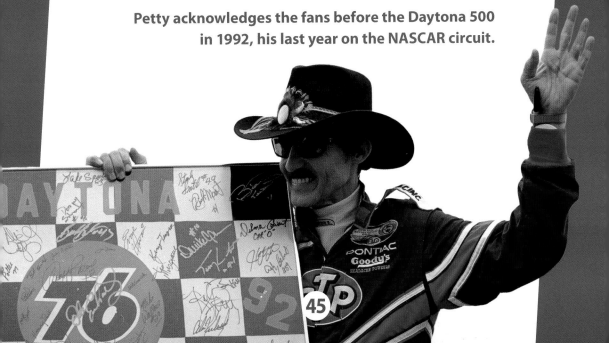

GLOSSARY

checkered flag
A flag of black and white squares that is waved when the winner of an auto race crosses the finish line.

complete game
A baseball game in which the starting pitcher finishes the game.

end zone
The place on a football field where teams score touchdowns.

expansion
The process of increasing the size of a league by adding new teams.

gold medal
The top prize at an event, most notably at the Olympics.

grand slam (baseball)
A home run with the bases loaded.

Grand Slam (golf or tennis)
Winning the sport's four major tournaments in the same year.

hat trick
Scoring three goals in a game in hockey or soccer.

no-hitter
A complete game in which a pitcher or team doesn't allow any hits.

par
The number of shots a golfer is expected to need to finish a hole.

reputation
How a person usually acts, as judged by others.

route
The path a receiver in football runs during a play in an attempt to get open for a pass.

streak
A consecutive series of events.

upset
An unexpected victory by a supposedly weaker team or player.

ONLINE RESOURCES

To learn more about famous sports records, visit **abdobooklinks.com**. These links are routinely monitored and updated to provide the most current information available.

MORE INFORMATION

BOOKS

Davies, Monika. *No Way! Spectacular Sports Stories*. Huntington Beach, CA: Teacher Created Materials, 2017.

Tejada, Justin. *Sports Illustrated Kids Stats! The Greatest Numbers in Sports*. New York: Time Home Entertainment, 2013.

Wilner, Barry. *The Biggest Upsets of All Time*. Minneapolis, MN: Abdo Publishing, 2016.

INDEX

ABOUT THE AUTHOR

Barry Wilner has been a sportswriter for the Associated Press since 1976, which may be a record in itself. He has covered every Super Bowl since 1987, and he has also covered nine World Cups and 13 Olympics. He has written more than 50 sports books.